Beauty
and the
Beast

Theme from Walt Disney Pictures' Beauty and the Beast

Music by Alan Menken

Lyrics by Howard Ashman

Arranged for Harp Solo,
Harp Duet, & Ensemble
by
Sylvia Woods

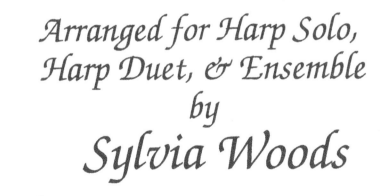

\-

Artwork by Heidi Spiegel

Visit us on the Internet at
www.harpcenter.com

ISBN 978-0-936661-49-0

Table of Contents

Notes from Sylvia Woods about the arrangements:

You may wonder why I wrote this book in two parts, with the first half in the Key of C, and the second in the Key of G. The purpose is to accommodate harps (and vocalists) with various ranges. For example, in the Key of C the "Easy Harp Solo" can be played on a small harp with a range of only one octave below middle C, and the "Advanced" versions need two octaves below middle C. In the Key of G, all the arrangements need a harp with a range going down 1-1/2 octaves below middle C, to the G that is the bottom line on the bass staff.

There is an interesting difference in the Harp Duets in the two keys. In the Key of C, the melody line in both harp parts is played in the same octave. In the Key of G, the melodies are an octave apart. The "Advanced Harp Part for Duet with Voice or Melody Instrument" can also be used as a part for a harp duet with the "Easy Harp Solo".

Sharping lever changes for lever harp players are indicated between the treble and bass clef staves. Pedal changes for pedal harpists are indicated below the bass clef.

For Harp Teachers:

As mentioned above, the "Advanced Harp Part for Duet with Voice or Melody Instrument" can also be used as a part for a harp duet with the "Easy Harp Solo". However, since the "Easy" part is the only one playing the melody, that player must be sure to bring the melody out so it can be heard. This may be a problem if the "Easy Harp Solo" player has a smaller harp, or has less experience than the "Advanced" player. If this is the case, it may be advisable for the advanced harp player to play the "Advanced Harp Solo" (pages 6-7 or 20-21) which includes the melody, instead of the versions on pages 8-9 or 22-23.

For Lever Harp Players:

In both of the "Advanced" harp arrangements in the Key of C (pages 6-7, 8-9, and 10-13), there is a B-flat accidental. If your non-pedal harp is tuned to the key of C (with no flats), you'll need to use your tuning wrench to tune the B string right below middle C to a B-flat in preparation for these arrangements. Then, before you begin to play, engage your sharping lever on the string, bringing the pitch back up to B-natural. In measures 15 and 38, disengage the lever to make the string a B-flat, and engage it again in measures 17 and 40, as indicated between the treble and bass staves of the music.

Key of C

Beauty and the Beast
Easy Harp Solo

Arranged by Sylvia Woods

Words by Howard Ashman
music by Alan Menken

This arrangement can be played as a solo, or as part of a duet with the "Advanced Harp Solo."
The lowest note in this version is the C one octave below middle C.

Key of C

Beauty and the Beast
Advanced Harp Solo

Arranged by Sylvia Woods

Words by Howard Ashman
music by Alan Menken

This arrangement can be played as a solo, or as part of a duet with the "Easy Harp Solo."
The lowest note in this version is the C two octaves below middle C.

7

Key of C

Beauty and the Beast
Advanced Harp Part for Duet with Voice or Melody Instrument

Arranged by Sylvia Woods

Words by Howard Ashman
music by Alan Menken

This arrangement is the harp part to be used with a singer or melody instrument. The melody is not included in the harp part. This arrangement can also be used as part of a harp duet with the "Easy Harp Solo."

9

Beauty and the Beast
Score of Duet for Advanced Harp with Voice or Melody Instrument

Arranged by Sylvia Woods

Words by Howard Ashman
music by Alan Menken

This is the score combining the Harp Part printed on pages 8-9, and the Vocal Part on page 14.
The notes of the Instrumental Part on page 16 are the same as the Vocal Part.

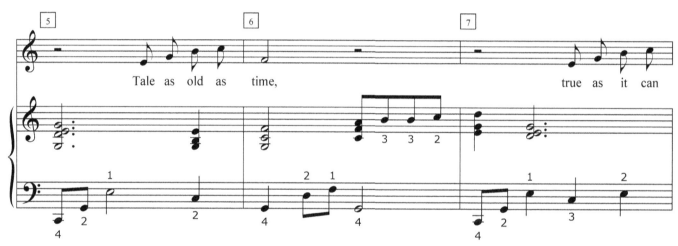

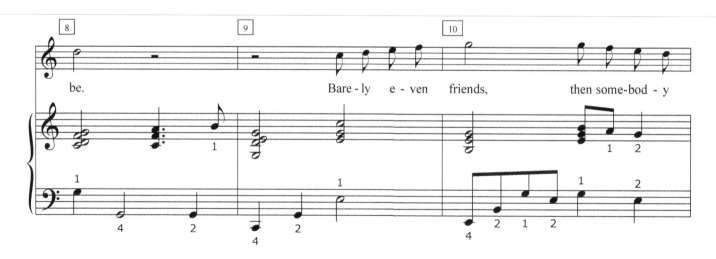

bends un-ex-pect-ed - ly. Just a lit-tle change,

Small, to say the least. Both a lit - tle scared, nei-ther one pre-

low B♭ low B♮

B♭ B♮

pared. Beau-ty and the Beast. Ev - er just the

same. Ev-er a sur - prise. Ev-er as be-

11

fore,   ev - er just as sure   as the sun will rise.

Tale as old as time.   Tune as old as

song.   Bit - ter - sweet and   strange,   find - ing you can

change,   learn - ing you were wrong.   Cer - tain as the

Key of C

Beauty and the Beast
Vocal Part

Words by Howard Ashman
music by Alan Menken

Arranged by Sylvia Woods

This Vocal Part is sung with the "Advanced Harp Part for Duet with Voice or Melody Instrument" on pages 8-9.
The score version of this duet arrangement is on pages 10-13.

14

Key of C

Beauty and the Beast
Instrumental Part

Arranged by Sylvia Woods

Words by Howard Ashman
music by Alan Menken

This Instrumental Part is played with the "Advanced Harp Part for Duet with Voice or Melody Instrument" on pages 8-9.
The score version (including lyrics) of this duet arrangement is on pages 10-13.

16

Key of G

Key of G

Beauty and the Beast
Easy Harp Solo

Arranged by Sylvia Woods

Words by Howard Ashman
music by Alan Menken

This arrangement can be played as a solo, or as part of a duet with the "Advanced Harp Solo."
The lowest note in this version is the G an octave-and-a-half below middle C.

Key of G

Beauty and the Beast
Advanced Harp Solo

Arranged by Sylvia Woods

Words by Howard Ashman
music by Alan Menken

This arrangement can be played as a solo, or as part of a duet with the "Easy Harp Solo."
The lowest note in this version is the G an octave-and-a-half below middle C.

Key of G

Beauty and the Beast
Advanced Harp Part for Duet with Voice or Melody Instrument

Arranged by Sylvia Woods

Words by Howard Ashman
music by Alan Menken

This arrangement is the harp part to be used with a singer or melody instrument. The melody is not included in the harp part. This arrangement can also be used as part of a harp duet with the "Easy Harp Solo."

23

Beauty and the Beast
Score of Duet for Advanced Harp with Voice or Melody Instrument

Words by Howard Ashman
music by Alan Menken

Arranged by Sylvia Woods

This is the score combining the Harp Part printed on pages 22-23, and the Vocal Part on page 28.
The notes of the Instrumental Parts on pages 30 amd 31 are the same as the Vocal Part.

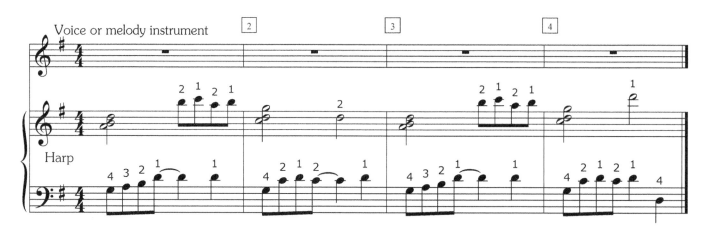

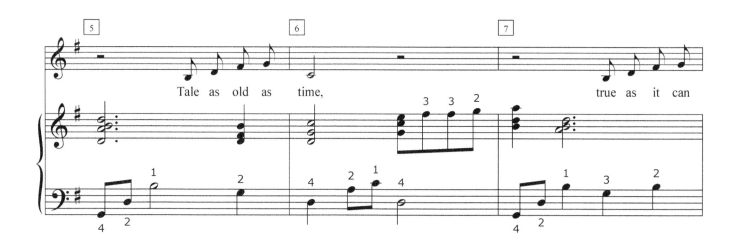

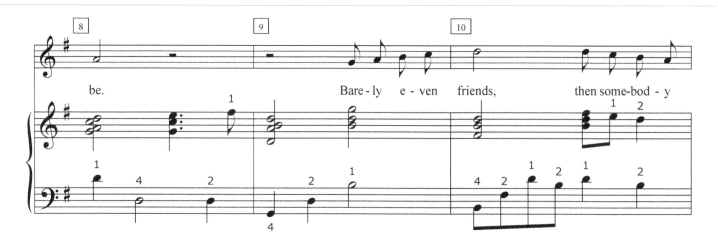

bends un-ex-pect-ed - ly. Just a lit-tle change,

Small, to say the least. Both a lit - tle scared, nei-ther one pre -

pared. Beau-ty and the Beast. Ev - er just the

same. Ev-er a sur - prise. Ev-er as be-

fore,   ev - er just as sure   as the sun will   rise.

Tale as old as time.   Tune as old as

song.   Bit - ter-sweet and strange,   find-ing you can

change,   learn-ing you were wrong.   Cer-tain as the

Key of G

Beauty and the Beast
Vocal Part

Arranged by Sylvia Woods

Words by Howard Ashman
music by Alan Menken

This Vocal Part is sung with the "Advanced Harp Part for Duet with Voice or Melody Instrument" on pages 22-23.
The score version of this duet arrangement is on pages 24-27.

Key of G

Beauty and the Beast
Instrumental Part - Low Register

Words by Howard Ashman
music by Alan Menken

Arranged by Sylvia Woods

This Instrumental Part is played with the "Advanced Harp Part for Duet with Voice or Melody Instrument" on pages 22-23.
If this range is too low for the melody instrument, use the "High Register" arrangement on page 31.
The score version (including lyrics) of this duet arrangement is on pages 24-27.

30

Key of G

Beauty and the Beast
Instrumental Part - High Register

Words by Howard Ashman
music by Alan Menken

Arranged by Sylvia Woods

This Instrumental Part is played with the "Advanced Harp Part for Duet with Voice or Melody Instrument" on pages 22-23.
If this range is too high for the melody instrument, use the "Low Register" arrangement on page 30.
The score version (including lyrics) of this duet arrangement is on pages 24-27.

Other Disney Harp Music Books
by Sylvia Woods

76 Disney Songs *for the Harp*
Music from Disney's **Frozen**
Music from Disney's **Tangled**
Music from Disney Pixar's **Brave**
Lava *from the Disney Pixar short film*
Up *Theme arranged for Harp*

available from harp music retailers and
www.harpcenter.com